# Out with the old.
# In with the new!

**Lila Hoxie**
Copyright © 2018 Lila Hoxie

D1517952

# DEDICATION

For my Friends
Hailey and Olivia

Rosie is 11 years old and loves adventure. She loves being in nature and listening to the birds sing and photographing what she sees. Rosie is a kind, curly haired girl who is about to start 6th grade.

Rosie has been best friends with Emily since preschool. Their favorite thing to do is watch birds from Rosie's treehouse. They even live across the street from each other.

Today is the first day of 6th grade. Rosie is nervous. As she walks into her new class she sees that Emily is hanging out with someone else! Her name is Hannah. Rosie knew that Hannah did not like her ever since third grade and Rosie has no idea why.

Even though Rosie is hurt, it makes her smile when she meets her new teacher, Mrs Brooke. She is kind and funny. Soon Rosie forgets about feeling left out and enjoys her class.

The bell rings. Everybody leaves. Rosie asks Emily if they can hang out after school and Emily says NO! She did not tell her why and Emily never keeps secrets.

She goes home and tells her family about her day and how nice her teacher was. Rosie decided to not tell them about what was going on with Emily.

Rosie goes to school the next day and meets a new girl called Jasmine. She is really nice and Rosie invites Jasmine to sit with her. They hang out all day.

Emily doesn't come over to her house for a couple of weeks but her new friend Jasmine does. They bake cookies and play with Jasmine's little brother. Although she is happy to have a new friend, she really misses Emily.

The last day before winter break Rosie realizes that she should give Emily some space and decides to focus on her family and making new friends. It's hard but she knows it is the right thing to do.

During winter break she was drinking hot cocoa and she saw Emily through the window with her new friend. It made her think about hanging out more with Jasmine.

On Christmas Day Rosie was opening her presents and she got a kindle. She was so excited. Jasmine and her family came over after dinner. They brought each other a gift and played with Rosie's new presents. It was so much fun.

After the Christmas break, everything seemed normal with Emily. They would smile at each other in the hallway and say hi. Rosie got great grades and had made a good friend in Jasmine. Sometimes it is good to have a change!

# THE END

CPSIA information can be obtained at www.ICGtesting.com
Printed in the USA
BVIW12n2017060618
518448BV00006B/13